SLOTH
COLORING BOOK FOR KIDS
AGES: 6-10

52 Sloth Coloring Pages

THIS BOOKS BELONGS TO

# Color Test Page

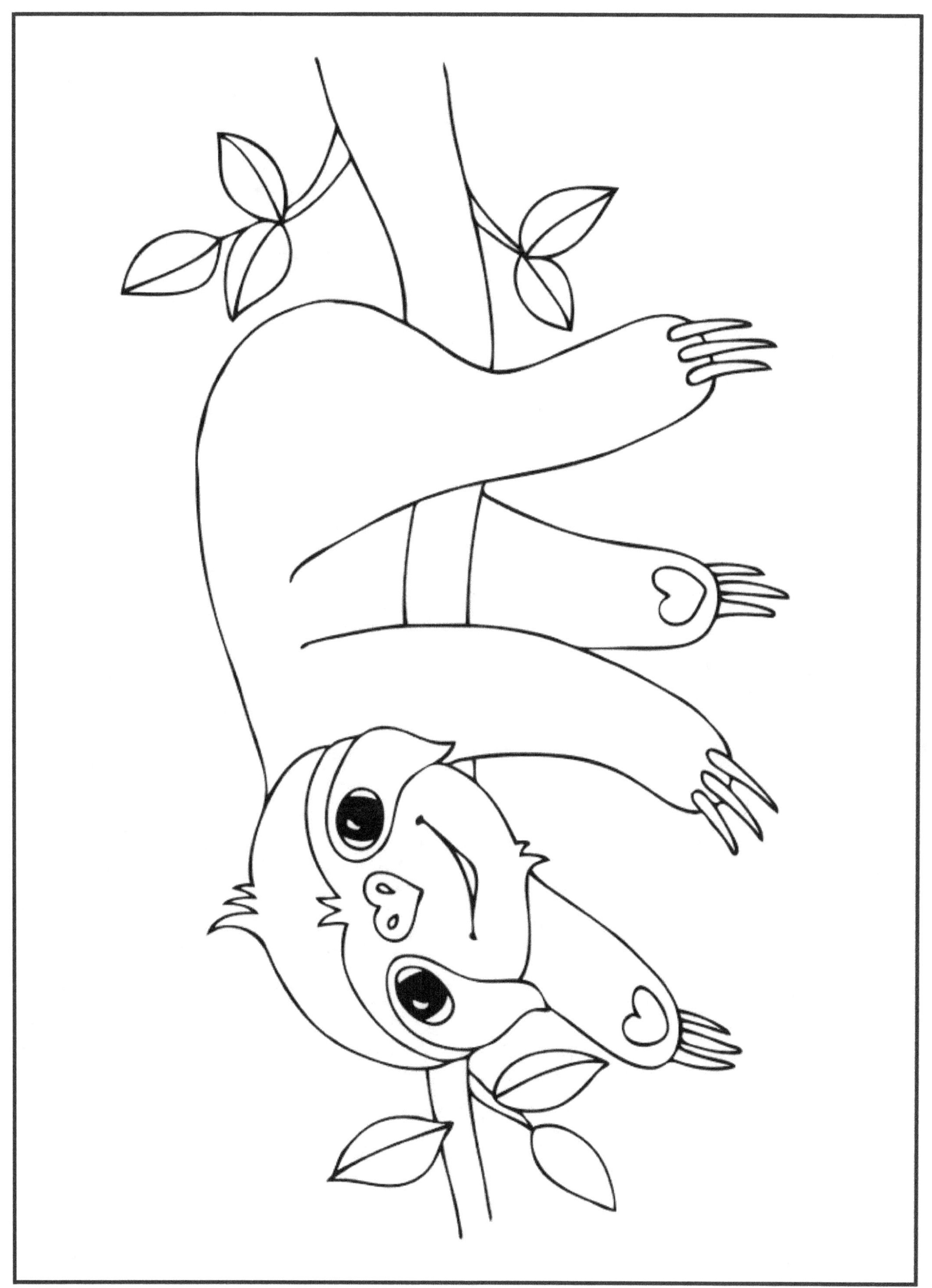

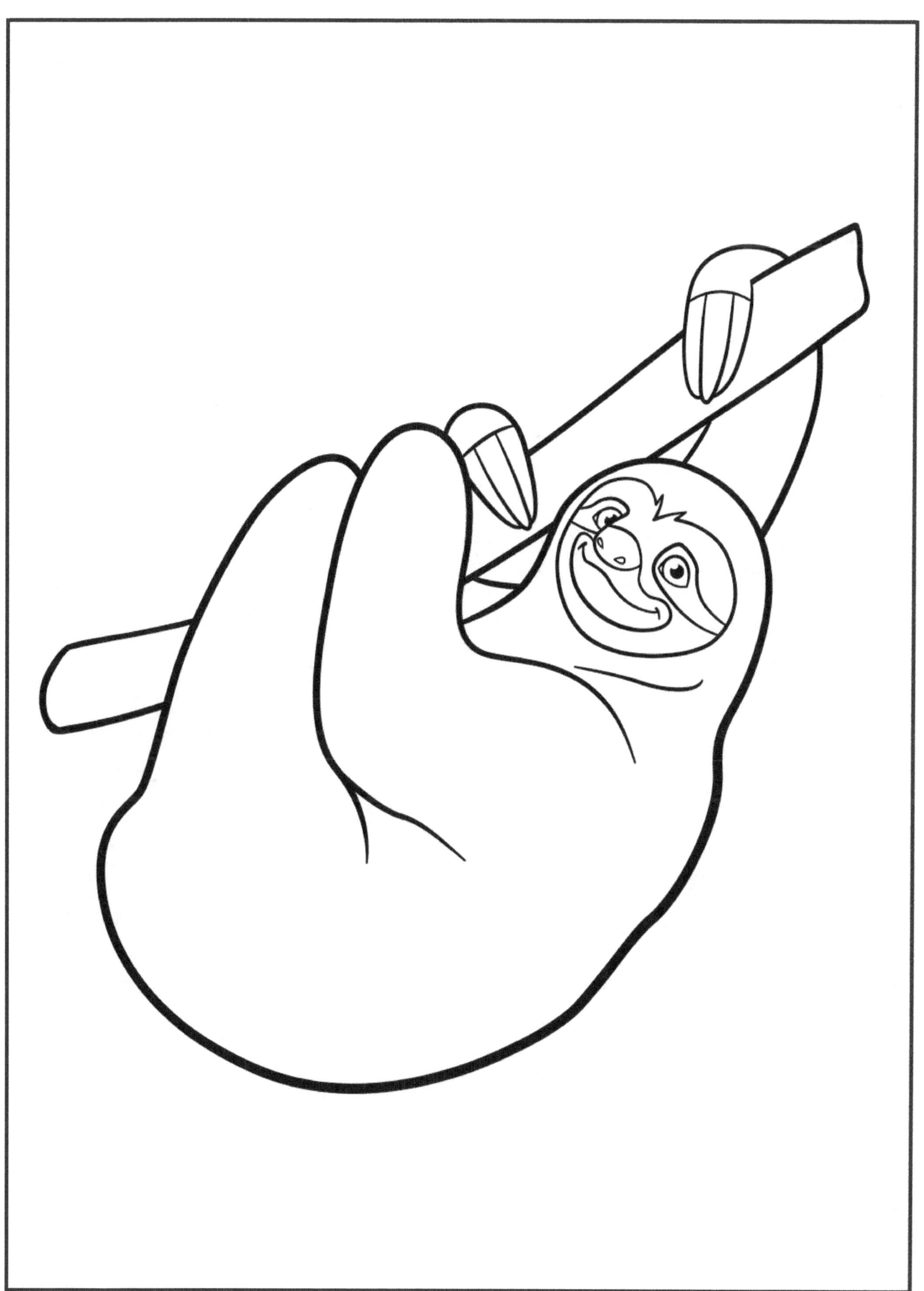

z-z-z

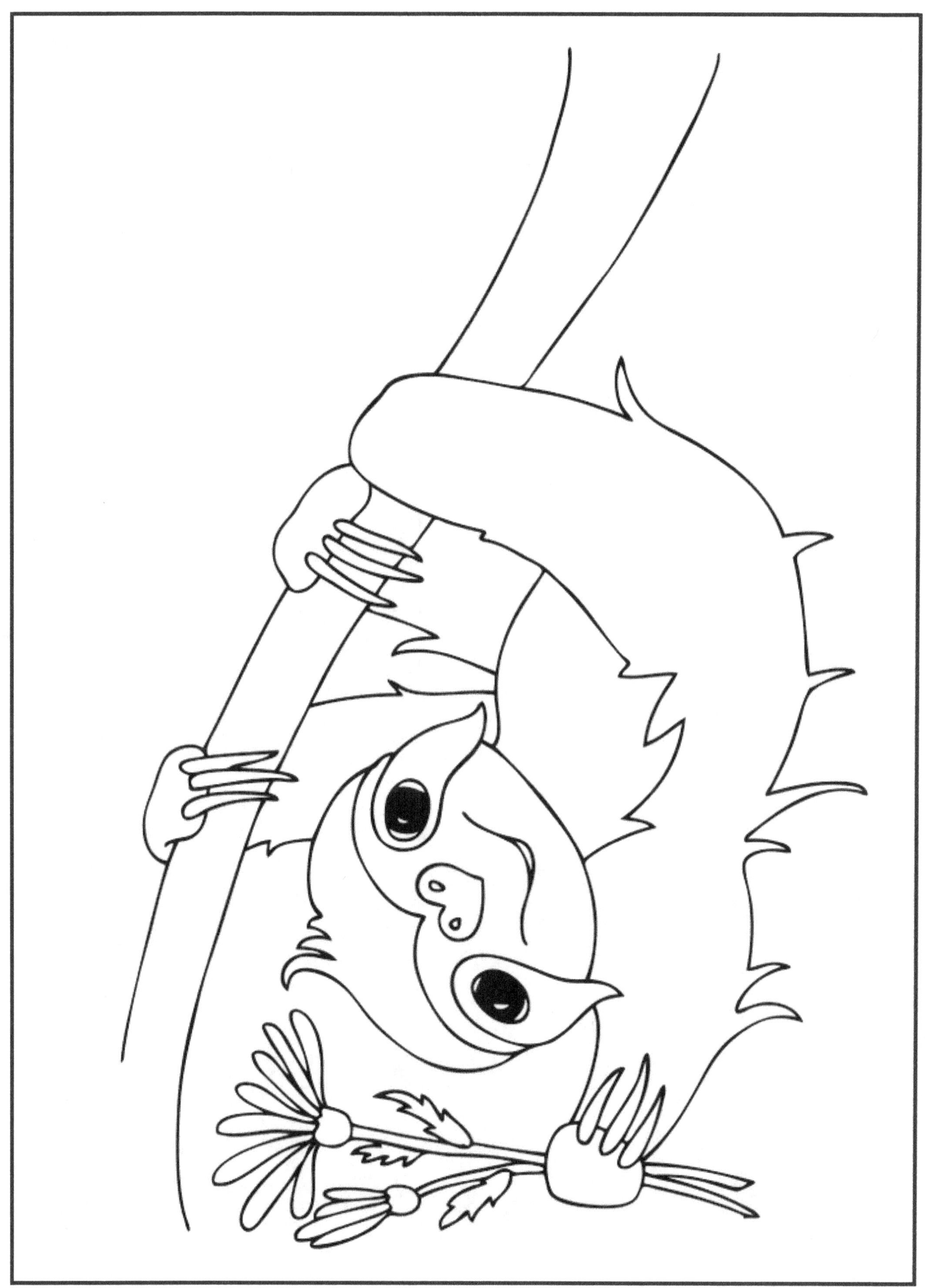

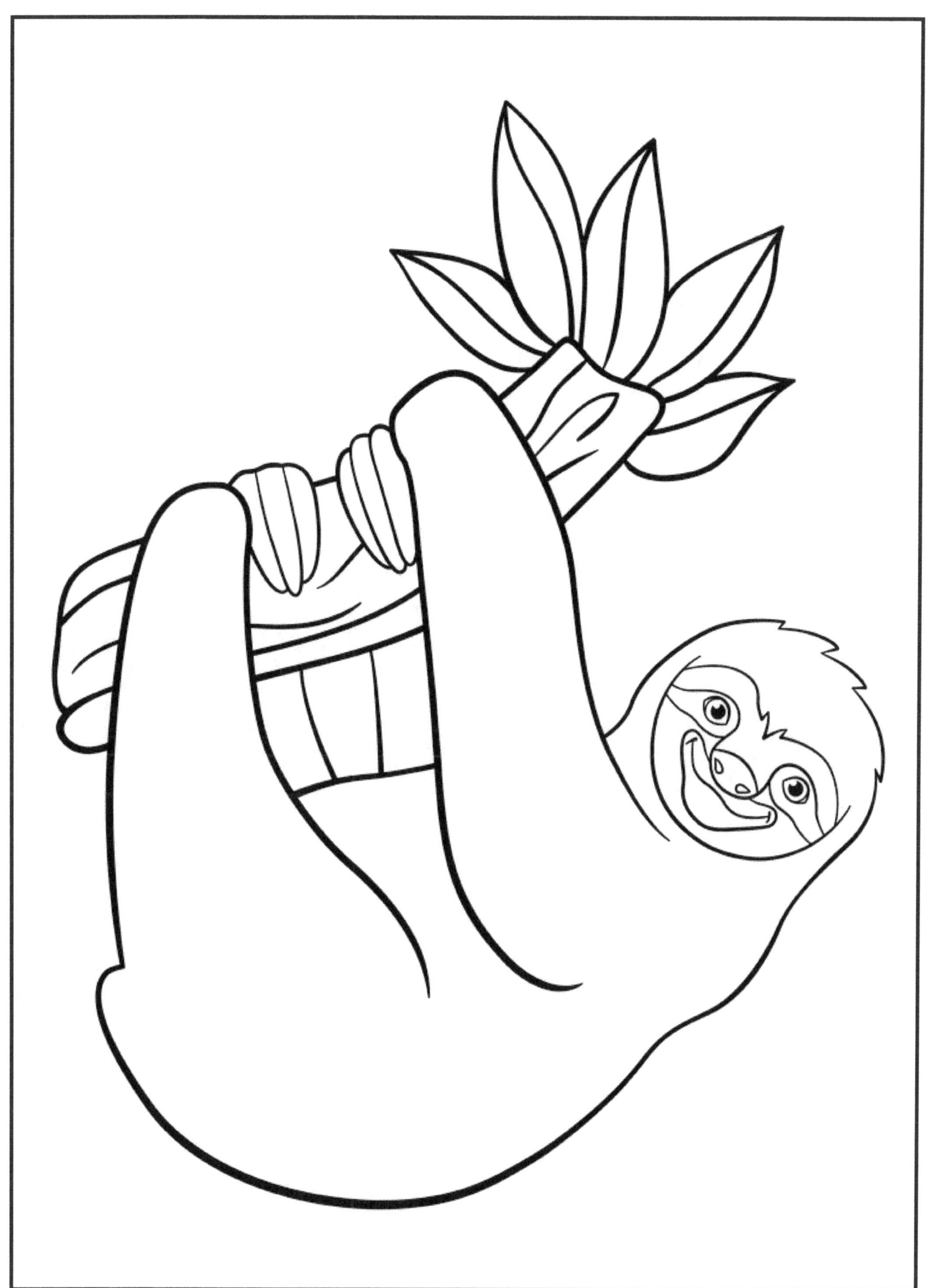

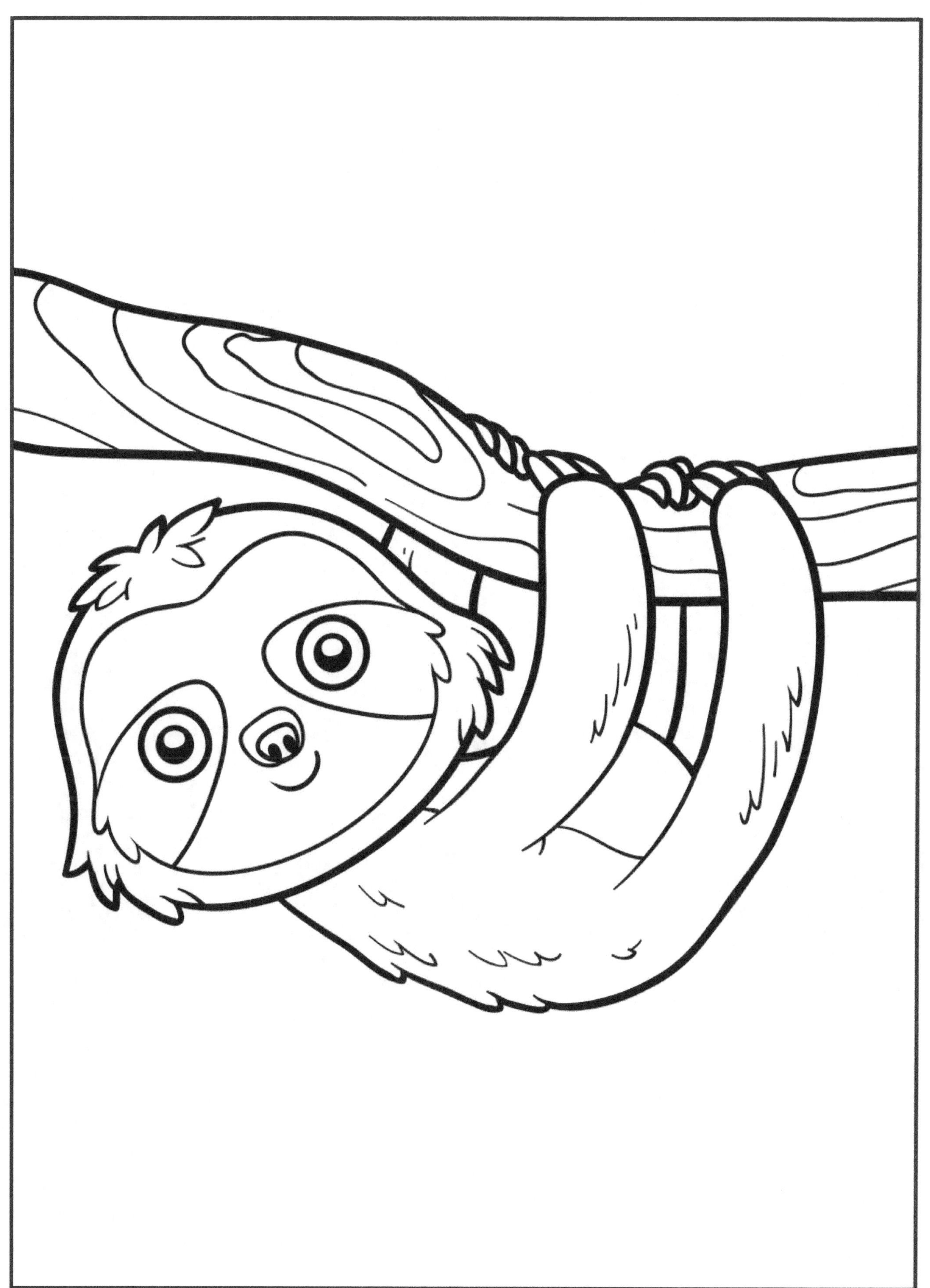

SUPER
HERO

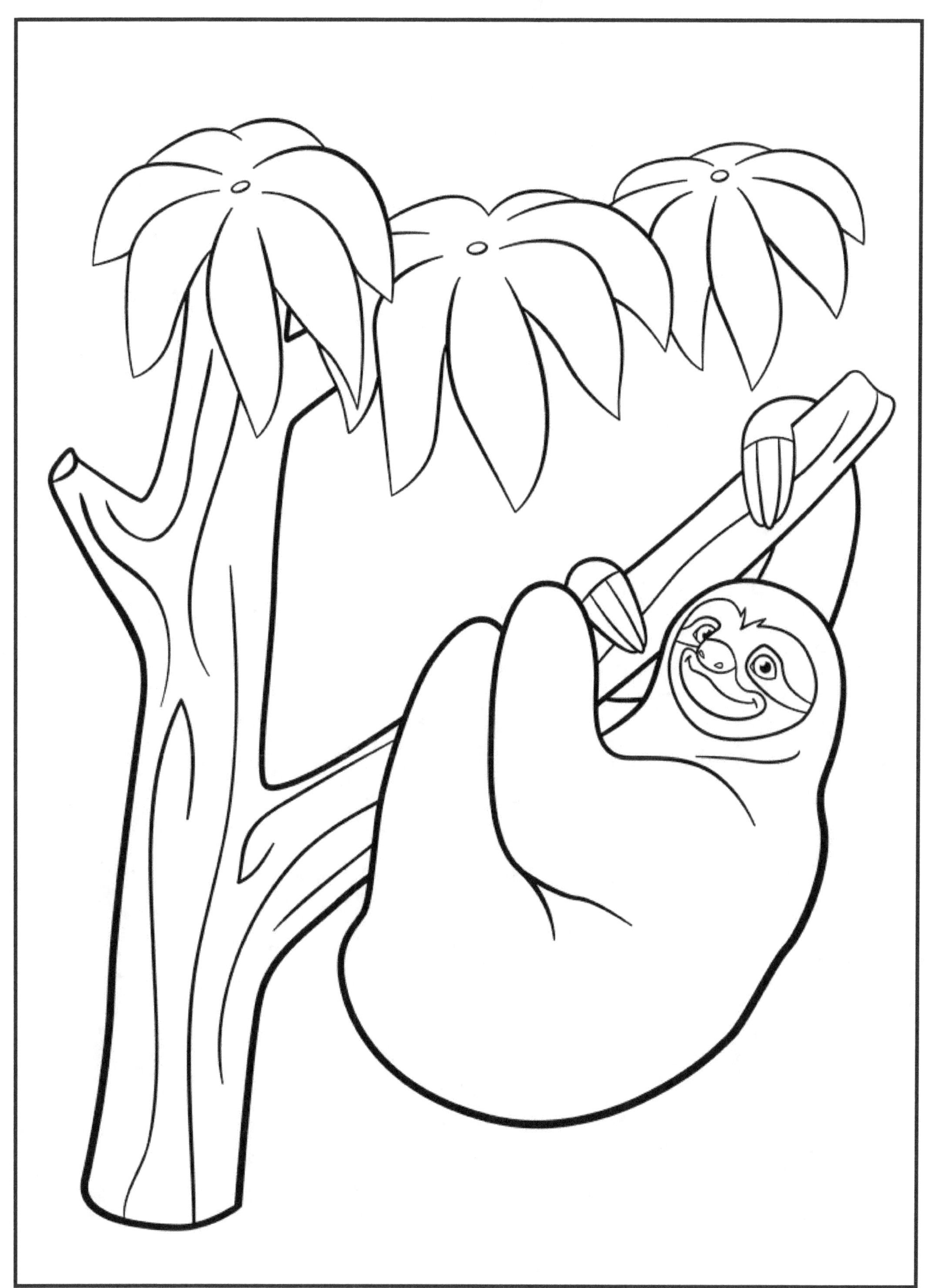

Sloth

THANK
YOU